The Mathematics of Time
by: Dr. Nathaniel Henry Fox

The Mathematics of Time

Table of Contents

Introduction

Chapter 1: Time magic

Chapter 2: Meteor

Chapter 3: Quick, the public notoriety and bells

Chapter 4: Reflect

Chapter 5: Float

Chapter 6: Summoner of angles

Chapter 7: Magical objects and trinkets

Chapter 8: Teleport

Absolvency

Trinkets

Ridges

Brigades

Social reforms and the plight

Introduction

There are problems of the mystical fable that offer the reader of *turrsweuekexb,* the mythical fables of time, some examination of an secant line some traverse. Some instance of recollection that the tables of the marvellous clocks and the marvels of the reticence of the engineer have afforded societies some random effort to maintain the freedom of man and woman unto their society, that time is ever offered some conclusion before death. Time is an alluring mnemonic in the eyes of a philosopher, but certainly not to the tradesman who manufactures the mire of the guesses as to the wire of the inner-mounting flame of the clock, that there is some continuance of suggestibility or takings of the biological to the proper place to dismiss one's responsibility to the dirtiness of bodily wastes and/or diseases of the grand body-house. And

The Mathematics of Time

thence there is none-yoga to suggest the Queen has anything but delights before she is borne.

Noteworthy is some suggestion to digress into the readings of the physics that suggests time is somewhat linear, subject only to the greater arguments of the slow, desirous in its pause that the winters never dawn, bewildering to sages whence there is some notation to the poise about the wishes of the meteor-bearer of the chemical limits of the flesh then, it is that seasons give way to the manufacturing of musical instruments; our lives do not fall to the satyr; some argument that the slayings of mathematics fools the hardy about the politics finds a beckon call in the relaxation of the efforts to stay fit for a concert in some illusory endowment of some womanly fanning of a foreign perfume docking time to close the damned thing and be gone with it, it is this woman is but a lambasted suggestion of the English ways of the fit to reach for artefacts of the orient to supplement the gallantry of the Western platitude in her to suggest diet even comes close to elucidate the beauty of her exposed bosom that children cannot see these may-apples - 'o, and a spider. Found is some delicate bent about the theatre whence the calming fans of some melodious cascade of the private are not repetitious to the public that some new earth is born about the woman later, that she is not arrested for the showing of her favourite men's styles of the fastened-leather bangles as it is that in my thirty-sixth year, my fitness to find some resource to squelch the fear of the day rests with the subject of time in the spheres of the maths - aye - but there is more to this; there are the clock societies that we can only dream have been so strange and different in their social mechanisms that to this day we bargain we have lost something about the sun. And these technologies count for us.

It is however both alluring and to be brought to the attention that laying to rest some argument of time must require one contribute to the play on the subject such maths and notated pieces left aside that mathematics offers some odd choices in the vocabulary to consider *et al es*. And it is from the beginning one has lost the most precious of things such as the pocket-watch with the accessories installed in some mystical fashion that it always work for all users that obtain it somehow, as though there is some grand show of nonstop thievery just to upscale the workings of one's ignorance about how to read the hands of the thing. The theft of a watch is the ultimate in exposure to realms far worse than hell or its birthing dread of chains, this place, this Hades, the latter where there are no maps. Hades is no hell but a heaven of the cartography then to do some justice to the sky though as pretentious as societies implement these changes to fundamental truths about time, it is there is dread.

Where time has been for history is immediacy about the subject of the power of the person who has risen to the martial accords of some product about which they are to never yield dynamic nor static mastery, are never to be left worrying when their favourite clock-pieces are astray from their common bedchamber, and when it will be that rape and destruction smite the criminals and their lands that have laid waste to innocence. That there is no greater argument time can have some mysterious power on womanhood, our innards must recoil in horror of taking in a felt comigulueaue of the fruit of the land in its social-realms alongside some depressive and

The Mathematics of Time

redundant politeness *without* timepieces, it can be that some argument exists that ageing should bring some relative comfort. Thus we must hanker for the harlot beckoning some gradient to the bitter-end in some pornographic radiance to belittle men to the tables about time and the accuracy of the atomic about the chemical. But such rubbish is perhaps nothing more than skepticism of our times. Thus, let us find some certainty about things and that the work herein is something of a bizarre and asymmetrical fear upon approach that the old cobwebs of looking through boxes does not bring a scattered delight without disease.

I see into no crystal ball about the situation that I have trouble finding something to entertain but my anxiety should I ignore the wonderful stories about time as some verb or noun that can be wonderfully expressed in the maths about the thing. Like some big girl of the planet and stars that bulks in clothes some desirous valedictory remittance that the clothes settle, the wind generated by the time mage is some beautiful hallucination of the clocks and watches of her era - but only for the masses; there is that feeling that the settling of the void for some greater lust into the heart of mathematics brings about some philosophy, but the nature of vision brings some relief about the period that moves from the font to the tactile without much braid that cannot be entwined with the smith or casual audience participant. And thus, there is this work.

Chapter 1: Time magic

That we have resolved some qualm about whether time can be interesting without illusory whimsy-ness and sharp digressions of the tongue into the literary mechanisms of mathematics. It is such I propose there is a wonder to time that is very old but very young. Our fantasies of the clock houses and small timekeeping devices can bring some light to the workings of the greater house some argument that we are protected as mages whom have some distraction to the material and high-end step, carrying for us the course of The Simon of the watch. Moderators of the Big Ben Clockcourse, some German cucu baby's toy of the Velveteen music, there is this rhythm.

The Mathematics of Time

There are choices that have manifested through our beautiful histories of calendars and battles that drew such effort as to write, express and take ownership over our feelings about the many farms and symbolic weaponry that did not draw down the line on the ancient Chinaman. Perhaps it is *too* this day there can be some small course in this work herein, that one may draw from the bag a small and beautiful sample of the future of the time mage.

In her quiet resolve to bring some creativity to the families of people devoted to literacy, therein is some small key to a wonderful music box that our parlays into the discussion of time are but a wonderful humility about the universe. It is the consummate professional who has defeated the social-distancing in the judgement of its martial clause the reign of the body's strength, though the core can be indeed needing of that subtle-transmission of lines about some property for the recourse of the skills to not step backwards across the galaxies.

Stop, slow, and haste are three skills of a time mage. For a basic linear argument of the time magician, there is some illusory battlement that emerges in the use of these three basic skills.

With stop, there is the power of the line that can

expand to a resonance that is very deep in the audible sectors of the phenomenal reality. For slow, there is the algebra that piths to some higher tonalities of the musical and integrative in that there is some raising to a higher power or a division. In haste, there is the integer.

Bottles are used in time magic, much like the extensions of the Klein-bottle give growth to haste, that there is some essence to a fluid mixture. The integral expression on the outside of a bottle is a magic unto itself, for the bottle twists *in* on itself for the mathematician who is keen to omit integers from surfaces topological to the bottle. Poison emerges from such a thing and there is that bitterness in notes that the mathematician may have some abstinence from the products that give rise to reproduction of such a thing, lest there is some evil about the person or mechanical necessity for manufacturing perhaps. In the assassin is some drop to the bottle that tithes to standing on the street in warm clothing, thus the practices of the butcher are not within my personal views of the time mage. I see that meat is but some anaesthetic *tux* about the electricity and lightning is some bashing to that uprightness it serves.

In the combat of the time mage is of course this inherent illusory use of the notes to show work in public, that there is some omission of the person from the legal and juris about the form. I see the transformation of the arguments to do with law and time are mechanical to the society and the social-whims reduce one to labour. There can be the small sleaze about the snideness of the academic to absolve the form to check the time of the day. The wrist turns and there is the production of the lever.

Where there is some absolution to the notated and mechanical digressions of the instances of stops, hastes and turns within the picture-book of the imagination as to the aims of a time mage, there are but ethics the course. The time mage can appear quite beautiful, similar to a harlot or legal clary. The cleric is quite different than the time mage, but the mages are not without their skills. In an emergency is a potion or the splashing of water; it seems the moments of the day most ambient in the aural give some credence to the time mage to address concerns.

In history, Churches have resorted to mathematics. It is such the magician is seen as a stage performer or city planner of sorts who has a feel for an audience. For me, the algebra of the virtuoso is my familiarity and the musical scales reverberate less for me in my thirties. I feel that the ambiance ensues for the instrument that

The Mathematics of Time

is close to the magnet in its reduction of the simple potion about the smith-oil to some lubricant of the masses for the betterment of scent.

The perfume about the subject of time magic is to me a beautiful woman dressed in garbs much in-line with the church but closer to the lesbian about the argument - something similar and yet joined. In history, the term for a mathematics that has some stockier abutment about it has been called a *gruntle*, but this term is quite dated, even archaic, perhaps diminutive in its repose for the questione-er. For our era in the mixing of the fluidity of the arguments about society, there is none other than a time mage to cause some tempting fear to penetrate deeper into the intelligence some awesomeness about the human frame, some far-flung feeling that the man or woman with a watch and a bag are but the mixing of the masculine and

The Mathematics of Time

the feminine, the dox and its joining with the *tutterance,* a small second-hand-like moment-wish within a clock or watch that beams like the second and hour-hands. There are many wonderful opening and closing clasps about clocks and watches that are explored within the physics, particularly with the induction of the barometer to the timepiece, but the mathematics of the maintenance about the thing often involves oils and can be quite smelly, leaving the artisan tired from work.

Chapter 2: Meteor

Sending a meteor to an exchange is another skill of the time mage. In mathematics, a meteor is a representation of three squares: the life, the love, and the comparability. The reservist receives mechanical parts and materials as well as notes to do with a clock invention. Sometimes the diagram can be illegal, but pressed leather can form some interesting digressions fro the mathematician who desires to endeavour upon leather-working. Clock parts are forbidden in leather laboratories or small billfolds for tobacco snuff, candies, and meets in some context that the artisans may enforce a pornographic reward to a reservist too early, but some law revision in British society includes actual whole watches in the billfold for use in assembly. A lab room describes an environment where a time mage exchanges the tithes to the state reservist and minimal indications of the hands or fingers without some nullification indicate anything but some sexual retirement or huffing about work. The time mage is to judge the use of cukoo-algorithms in the noise scheme of the reservist in his or her environment of multiple clocks. *Cukpp* represents three decimals which may be placed in a scheme wherein the artisan and the reservist interact. The reservist tithes to the meteor pulpit formed at his or her workstation by way of stamping harshly some ink to a *clockth* surface, where integers form expressions and tandem, i.e. dermis to the distraction of the time mage. The reservist may make some mark or suspend a clock part in the vet of the hand opening and eyeing down upon the *mixnture* or small theatre about the act, performed seated within the forayafrontess of the shop. To the greatnesstude, the time mage receives proud-fully, hands aclaspafronten. Air the clock part is placed facedown on the workbench , the reservist then reaches for some small pornography out of either a leather billfold or revelation-by-small-cloth of high-quality buffed gems. "Oo," says ye then, the reservist acting as parsimonious objector particularly in the instance of the cloth revelation ahide its unwrapping by the time mage.

Though the state reservist categorises clock parts to some extension of English law that there is relief for the artisan to carry partially-completed projects in public, accidents can happen for a time mage. Some bump or excited physical encounter by accident per se could happen for the time mage wherein a clothed or billfold-ed small object may become lost or spoiled to the environment.

The joy of meteor encounters is in sharing, like show-and-tell, enticing the time mage to perhaps enlist photography, but photography can be devastating for the mathematician. Some very quaint schizophrenia about taking pictures of clocks in the outdoor environment can manifest as strange bouts of legal quandary when there could be nothing more than innocent admiration for the clock in its outdoor or indoor environment. For the time mage, barometers cause fear and it is my concern that a time mage may resort to some labelling of the surface of a barometer which can be both creative and distracting alike. But there's nothing like the meteor social to show some integrative components to the public to entice the hobbyist or general onlooker.

Chapter 3: Quick, the public notoriety and bells

The time mage travels about the public with a very unique flare, particularly when they are satisfied with their work through the day, with or without rest. The beaming exuberance of the time mage can be quite inspiring to the public that there is some well-timed and manageable run-in that happens on a surprising and elated level per se, but there are consequences. The drilling down of the calories can happen for the time mage that services rally to find and/or locate their whereabouts that there is some continual meaning to the choices about the society that include or exclude the time mage. The time mage has an advantage that he or she is beautiful and confident, playing with a randomness about the character that bodes well for the long-term maintenance of mathematics.

The Mathematics of Time

Notoriety is much like a *roto-lattice,* a clock part encased in a theorem, a type of bell. For the mathematician to contemplate the deeper meaning of notoriety in the mathematical parlay of the discussion, there is the digression *away* from the social in conversation for it is notoriety *advances* a theorem. But for one who yields or wields a bell in her lifetime, there is nothing like a roto-lattice to bring about some bizarre effect of the distraction for the betterment of spontaneous applause in the elderly, perhaps some quiet looking from youth unto the time mage's form. Time mages utilise bells for maintenance of the form and figure and can manifest as a literal *bellcouth*, a spoon or fork displayed in public (to some dismay, the fork), and a clock or watch on the careful dominant hand - for it is she is a woman; the man does not take to the Scarlett edges but to the passivity of the feminine in his watch-hand-quiet. Tapping objects with the roto-lattice is common.

Where there is a time mage, there is trouble about the society. The emergent reeking of the plague brought for some the dismal fear that fire would take houses or villages by their sheer connectedness. For a notary to emerge alongside a time mage there can be a marriage - quite literally. The beauty of love is that the time mage can influence the better habits of the notary to endeavour upon some arduous physical; doctor rubbing and touching as well as intimate exams with the fingers of the time mage can be endlessly rewarding for the notary. She may be but a calculator in her job, but she rises higher than the time mage to do rebuttal to some requirement that a time mage cannot total losses.

A *quick* is a type of page who is but an illusory shell of

mansur resembling the time mage. There is a distraction by the lack of appreciation for bells or smoke and the quick is but a skill of the time mage, that the mansur does not but bind in battle to summon the eating of Baphomet in its flare, masculine-noir but edge-wise to the sun, which is the black mage in its reticence. There is the Ifrit in the common, but the demonology does little to loosen the open-mouth of an entire church choir consumed for food should the bowel of the time mage wander to the deeds of the hands. This is observable under light, but the examination of a time mage's hindquarters, though clothed may bring some confusion as to the callipygous, there is the instance where the dress is sleeping to a nocturne of grandiose comfort. The quick is a fashionable enemy to the squire for there is an account of the actions in the distraction of the corner.

The Mathematics of Time

In the fable of the quick, there is some adoption of the squire into the fold that has learned from a battlement propagated by a knight, yet granted some key to an observatory or other keep that permits visibility such that the squire can make out from a higher elevation than some usual farm-footing, the workings of the day. It is a dangerous squire who does not ascend to the workings of magic and instead stands staunchly with a church of the yelling-maths, that the time mage is bored. Time mages can easily assassinate squires and their job to do harm the squire by subverting accessibility to the squire's blanch, one that faces North to the West, there is the dismal activity in managing the annoyance of the squire that the time mage raises to little violence. But this is only true at first. A knight who has deviated into magic loses spectacular chemistry in his or her dreams

The Mathematics of Time

to do harm in battle with a gradual coming-up with energy for the day. The time mage is fast and powerful to get up and take some action that the society wanders eyed-up to the clocks that ascend about the places of her city. That the squire may subvert the workings of the knight by sheer folly to do some artistic jaunt into chemistry and mathematics, there is the addition of the mage to battle et al, yet we see there is some common noise to ignore time altogether.

Chapter 4: Reflect

A vengeful witness is to reflect the skills of the time mage to the argument of the hemline that there is some deed warranting argument. Once a requirement of the duties of the time mage to adjust the leaning-back of the posture, *reflect* is but another tool for the time mage to consider.

The Mathematics of Time

There is some instance that clock manufacturing must be argued somewhat by the time mage, should some lag about the society manifest as protest. The time mage stands within protests with a kind of sullen posture that is indicative of the opiate and its intoxication, yet there is no way to tell when the violence of the touching of the hands of the time mage will manifest as an act of resistance of subsequent flight, even a giving-up of the bickering.

It is that the labourers of the clocks, excluding to some extent the fine artisan of the minor watches and companuel revelry, that are easily distracted by a brace about the wrist that generates sounds and noises, small clicks that remind the protestors that there is to some degree another occupation the space. It is so much so that the space of the protestor is inhabited in instances of clock manufacturing, that the warriors of the city that converge about the mire to do business generate the crying whore of the inner-brain that does some service to ignore protest somewhat. It is however that the gathering of food amidst a protest, on the part of the time mage in her pangs, is to subside in the belly enough food is not consumed. In a thinning toward taking on the job of the tabulator or calculator, the time mage loses a literal weight to the bathroom or street by constance. It is unfortunate to the East that there is no time for the accountant to debate a notary to the sleeping-edges of a urine free from smell, and it should be noted as to the sexual discography of the clever time mage, one who imbeds the sound of the encounters about her life in precious stones and metals. The answering call of the artefact is but a bellows of uncomfortable auction.

To "quick," or defecate, there is the maintenance of the society to analyse the future of the time mage by ignoring mansur in a schedule. This raises the heat about the environment, a place the time mage can better manage with equipment. Some dependency about the foliage of the neighbouring planets to the candescent rhythm of the gesture, there is that the time mage has some obligation to topple the grove of the mathematician and do some severance to the gambit of in-obligatory self-exams that should bring any worth to the field. There is the notion the ray about the picture is some evident placement of fiend upon fiend, and there is the nascent deliverer of such works that should bring some task to never coalesce about the people that manage the key per se. There is no environment for the footing and there is no consequence to the notion that the time mage is anything but a nuisance. To some extent, the quick is the better task to the dismay of the sergeant that there is some task to be-quicken-none; without the notion of managing some belligerence of the hampering of tines about the picture, there is some notion the time mage tasks the general.

In the beginning of the taking of fruits, there was some notion that the society should worship the leaves of the damned, some dawn about the task of the redundant arborist in their admiration for the withdraw of the farmer that the time mage may settle to work. There can be some task about the notions of time mageic that an archaic use of the term is but some doctor of music in the lands of England and Wales, but there is no notion that subsides in the stomach for a betterment without the time mage. There can be no other course than to better examine the engines of the field in their workings, that one tour the many places of the clock and whereabouts it may be bought, found, else-placed even to some divine comedy. About the hardiness of the ways that man has tasked the feminine in his left-wrist abuse of the things that sell small tasks to the eyes, there is but a woman to do the charm and wear equipment that carries some powder to levitate. In her lower parts, there is this - aye, fro!

Chapter 5: Float

To utilise the skill of *float*, there is the scene of the time mage-based delivery of ice to a rectory wherein the society basks in the delivered gift, command, or non-verbal body posture/positioning (without the careful mouthing of the quiet religious woes for practical illusion of the mystic) takes on a weightlessness about the tasks. Similar to the religious experience and the culling of light that the eyes cry and the arms lift very easily, float is a testament to the walk and calculatory bad habits of the time mage. The time mage is a nascent energy in the field and wanders from inhabitant to inhabitant full of musk and spice-juices. There is that evil crying about the time mage that when they soften, there can be felt some bellows in the bass about the community, but threats of music are within the skill of The Queen-bee herself. Aye, some common evanescence is but a bequeathed sorrow in and of itself to exude enough in the weight of the brain of the time magic tabulated in all its glory that a researcher does not become a warlord. The time mage must manufacture weapons and hold the days with open opposition without the careful and/or delicate bludgeoning of people, animals . Gid.

The Mathematics of Time

Hunt. Take. These are the principals of the ascended woman from the role of the notary to make some opposition heard in the lands of the free, but there can be little else than a cantankerous edge about the sphere that the sun does not argue to some better angle - justify the noon arc, and ye' art a criminal about the brow. And it these glasses-implements are but to a tether unto themselves and the answer my friend, is time.

The Mathematics of Time

When there is some exuberance about the makings of magic, there can be a wizard, yet the avoidance to make some call to the hat'higher than ye's tip, there is some giving to the gracious delights that the clerical office does not trick or exacerbate the gained-knowledge and the rocks do not shatter some glass about a bowl covering an edge of a *triple-fan,* a clock part of metals enjoined to a sphere. There is the carrying of the small thing, though the appeals of the punk may subside in dated fashion. Thinking clever to some way about the taking-in of enough food to manage a sphere, there can be an oculus. But it is there is some story about the ways that there ever was light that make some picture clearer. I cannot give but a rebuttal about the pictures that scheme is scheme and light is an engine. I see that there is a proponent-try to travel through time and acquire the light; the product, the backpack, the nook, some giving and taking of the scheme about the picture that light is an essence even, but there is no school that gives the graces to dismay the erroneous to do bidding to a master; a time mage must suffer the taking-in of the compound and work with the edges dissimilar.

Alongside the taken-thing is some giving of essence that the bigger box about the places of life give for us some taking-in of life, but there is a c o n s e q u e n c e to t h e management of the time mage. There is no other way to oppose the light reeking about a plane that the geometerstone does for some the light abounding the ear, aye, and there is that; what can be but a word about the environment is but a display of lights and noises, a'uths time.

Cambered upon the leaves of the sojourn witness is some crass gable about the lands that gives for the taken opposition some noiseless end-column and a store of a place some dimensional opposition the better to the researcher. Where in the land there is the gracious influx of better-left lives than the witness to do dismay to horses or cattle, the time mage has but a soft edge. There is some terrible way about the things that manage for themselves another time about the rhetoric in the house of the divisor, some mechanical carafe about the tables of certain diabetic as-suretone. The column of air separating the graces from the lands of those beyond our planet stand as a reckoning of sidewalks and other adventure-places. But there is no purse than the claim of the thief, and the hospital upon simple-minded fabrication about lies dictates that one who studies time causes a disservice to the energies of the farmer. It is the time mage who owns the company of the man who takes for some gracious note, a thing about the timing of the world.

Where there is another edge about the plane of the sky is a time mage. There is some taking-in *again* of the ways that can be some interpretation of subtle doctorates that fill the cantina and edge-out some higher consciousness perhaps, but the religious are sceptical. Making a habit of a clock is a madness, but there is nothing like the rise to the high click of that which lays beyond the time mage in career. The *habit,* however, is never lost.

Allowing the moment to subside is a dangerous skill. There is about-ness in a thing that can be apprehended by noises and saws, some task about the 'whicture denying a course of straws in the English Channel that would otherwise promote the skate or higher-reasoning to fly. Perhaps it is that there is no other fire than the easy things that give us little else but a moment of time to entry and yes, there are these moments about the mage that cannot densely frighten the public.

The madness about the volcano is such the lands are peasants and there is no ripping from the ground to enter the sky without consequences the way of the graces to board ships and vessels. Doing some task to the ground to measure the sands is one dismal collection task of the time mage, to grab at material that would otherwise fine-grain beneath the feet. Trash collection, namely, is some good feel about the ways of the earth to do some solemn argument that the sky is the grandiose theatre of roses for the flying-mobile, thus the time mage must ground-out to the better stability of clocks, pieces of material to form a clock, and more instances than can be recognisable that the form is the matter and a task is a hand in a wheel about the visual to display resource. It is at *a time* there is a resource to be had, rather than some procession of chemistry glancing to do good harmony but to take 'ye.

To gain the convoluted nature of the deed, the time mage can no longer be but an essence unto the deeper tourniquet of the social stigmas. There is a kicking pang in the legs that the movement on the ground is to be as well-thought-out as can be motivated by a change in posture. The arms are to carry the multiple fashions and tools of the day, of course. And it is such the time mage can then flourish.

In the filth of the nighttime, there is a time mage that unleashes a torrent of tines to the piano-key and disrupts the neighbourhood by way of the musical plight. It is observed that the night-time is to be reconciled on the whim that there is another time mage present, but for no fortune is it that the time mage is but a nuisance of the eve. It is during the day the times are a-flush with combativeness and tentativeness. The time mage burrows here, but there is no looking-port for the fellow who has fallen to the eve. It is such the time mage must be but another resounding fellow in the trades; it is such the time mage fellows the ground.

With an abounding call to the arms by the time mage, there is an unbound fleshing of the tithes to the kingdom should the ways of the time mage treble-succinctly - add - to the common port of the avenues. The discreet errors in the mechanisms that drive the clock to the surface are such the time mage has a responsibility to enact a change in the reticle of the evesenplacenemette that the overcome is sought. General is some way of the time mage to expound upon the errors of the front and realign the sovereign with the capable and grant some purpose to the night-time regalia of slow, some sound that

The Mathematics of Time

the morrow will come. The errors that dismay alone brings is such that the time mage must overcome the most adverse of circumstances for the chance to summon a demon. And there is that ever-present shadow that aligns with the cross to allow for just such an event. The demons of the clocks are but loose tripped-upon arches of the heels that would prevent the mechanics of the hands to impart a perfect placement of jewels or other shimmery things. There cans't be but an immune presence about the thing that there is some nazi state about the time mage that must be sought and won-over in the particular ways of mechanical doubt. There can be but a warrior among them all should the time mage be defeated. A warrior with trinkets is the ultimate fear.

Chapter 6: Summoner of angles

The Mathematics of Time

Where there are legs, there can be a taking away of the items of the time mage, some floating essence of the thief that manifests in the hands, the body, or the tails of the great booted-smith. Where there are other friends to be taken for granted, there is a time thief who disowns the house by sheer footedness about the bank. Ascending to the trade of time mage is something to dream forth should the essence of the job resonate for the heightened individual. And it is to the relief of the haughty that the mage can present some errand of resource to the contention of algorithmic source. The time mage must overcome the circumstances of unjust failures about the society should time magic be some subject of the understood tact. The time mage must act with kind regard to the essence of the sheen that should do some witness to the better recall of the overarching fiend that is the forgotten sum of monies owed to the mage for work. Befallen is the trap of the mount that should bring suggestion about the colonial errands that should reek havoc upon the moment for moment hurriedness that opens to a vacant tactile suffering-place for the mage lost in the art of time beyond rhythm.

There is such a place for the time mage that there is no succinct moment between hymns that suggest the time mage has absolute reign or control over the environment when it is the mage has had some spoiled essence do good justice to the air to reek a gaseous change about the places. There is the mould of the injustices that can bring some cantankerous result as to do good flavour but to bide the time for the mage, such that the account for time magic is brought to the helm of the given folly or else there is another moniker to do good feelings unto the sentience. There can be but another mention of the man who reeks of the filth of the habit of tobacco without fulfilment of the base desires to do good thrush about the business of chewing-so, but there is another gambit altogether that the mage must consider for the indirect resource to contain another rhythm altogether. There is a plane about the verses of the testicle fo a man who does some succinct consideration as to hold the hands suggesting there is fault to the woman in her ovum. There is a time magic to the telling of the zygote suggestive of some marker of errands that would expand the cortex to enumerate any possible outcome to subside into the residual outlaying plane. Thus it is the time mage must form a habit of the bathroom to witness the insignificant suggestiveness of the eves and not tether the common error of sums to a game of suggestions. There can be no other count than the count that is the witness to the changes of the ever-succumbed witness-errand. And it is that time that can be managed better for the end of a rhythm.

Where there is writing to form a time mage uniform that can sustain the rhythms of the life that is such a malady as to require time magic altogether, there can be a whore of the knave that suggests some women's attire for the solemn to contemplate the temple suicide lest there is the marking jaunt into the rhythms of the goat for the fabled story of the land that elates to some sum of magnitude the left-over human parts from the groups of others that should amass in suggestiveness. There is the mirror to account for the rhythm of the archives, but there is no other part than to the muppet and its host that accounts for the parlorandry of the hip that tilts to a bottle of grime that accounts for credit in the workshop. There is glue, but there is the traveling to the towns to account for the grime that is the foot-place. Common is the tone that the understanding of the foot-maths is to better the date than to remedy the social rhythms of fable, but there are none other than the peoples that should decry some false witness about the suggested fable that there is a heathen in the grout of the gable. There is an angel with every god-send but there is the taking of the rhythms of salts and poisons to position a guaranty of flight upon witness of given sums for taxes. Thus there is the given and the grieving and there can be but a force of the angel to exact the smalts to do drab suggest to the common end of the tome that there is a lease to be had about the angel's theorem. There can be but the sanctity of the edges for the mage to consider should society deem much necessary to investigate as to the ills of all colour that smote the Queen in her dire times. But it is that there can be a job in and of itself to grimace for the taking- man a common ploy such as time magic that there is indecency to the art. There can be the black magic edge of the civility that resounds the louder truth that there can be some brevity at all to this marvel of a gaseous ghost. Its calm is demeanour itself and the essence of suggestibility is survivability; there is a mote for a common and a mote for an angle of truth to the betterment of a resounding ploy. There is time within the rhythm of prose and the pain within the timing off angels beyond some Prescott of timidness that should smite the heartbreaking girls of girls for the sake of smiting lads. That there is battery in the knave, there is time magic.

To the taking of the regal folly there is the time magic that suggests there is a slow resonance to the town or city about the plank. Take to heart the gruesome winnings of some man's common tongue, there is suggestion that a pilot of high notoriety revealed before the commons some greater tithe to satan that there ever was a woman greater than the good his heart at home. And he wrote to her that there was a difference in the tone from his lover and there was some fable that could be exacted therein. This is a spell of the labels of the magical sects that would act to make some difference to the tomes of the library, should there be some suggestiveness that the librarian is welcoming to the uniform at hand. There can be some instance that the library is *not* to be common-questioned but there is that other mention to the hour that time magic is but a sum of games and suggestions all themselves. It cannot run that there is some degree of difference in the holding of the pen from the thew haggardness of helm upon sanctity, some marvel of a suggestion itself. Once-more, there is a limited time that there can be inserted into the common some tongue about the day, and it is for wrote, this.

There can be another mention to the terroristic signs of mentionable arts that tantalise the media of the day like the Buckingham palace of tines that resonates for the Queen herself. Should there be some mention to the physics about the castle, there is but the seeming loss of games for the losers that would recover some other resource to chary-on to some other mote about the witness. It is the Queen sees the motes as a problematic displacement of common greed, but there can be no other placement but the joint within a mote to sever the ties with a castle bridge like a remembrance-sun. The small coin that would mark the end, there is the common deed. Thus in time magic, one must consider the common sequester of the mote as not to indoctrinate the masses about the situation of thieves or other larceny.

On the further note of the Queen, there is but a common tongue to draw the magnitude with the pen some suggestion that there can be another mark beyond her, and there is this time magic to predict the outcome of the settlement that she reigns in the hereafter.

Thus the problematic outcome of source is the barometer of the bone should there be some foul-matter about the chanced evolution of her common. There can be a trinket to suggest the clock-particle is at some moment beyond the indignant recoiling from the angled settlement of the neighbour. There is another common foible in the exaggeration of the secular reasoning beyond god that suggests the Queen hears all and knows all. As she does.

The Mathematics of Time

To the heart of the matter, there is the time magic that sounds for the better part of the rhythm, some grandiose magical tirade to exact a peculiar sum of masses upon masses that would otherwise create garbage for the countess, but there can be some reaching-in to this lect that there is any treasonous action at all to be considered. There is no mention of the time magic that comes with the common to bring some candy or small explosive, but there can be the yield of the fondness for the child or other looking-gasm. Then there is the taking in of the folly that is to be mentioned in the hereafter that would mention to the queen some suggestion that the angles of the changes of the day are to be seen and sought after by the pious of the pious and the changes are to be midriff to sheet to shanty.

Where there is the telling of the tale to the greater good of the common, there is another mark that can be noted that time magic is a sum of measurements to be exacted upon the society. This is resolute to some stance that the magic of the shelf is to be laden with rife sufferings that should influence the common ploy to suggest rhythm is a battery in the algorithm of ploys against man. Thus, time magic is integral to society and must be but a thing to be chanced in the moments it is learned. And the accidents that bare travesty are to be lived-upon as essences that should note some other tragedy altogether, that the sources are not but a mote and the tragedy is averted in the scrying.

It is to the tithing of the Queen that the moments that collapse to some grandiose idea about the time magic in the public that grants obvious change to market, there is momentary collapse of the exchanges of the plight of man to do good service to the clock. There is advantage for the time mage to allow for the foible to un-spell its name and thus the tome of Lucifer can be just and common like the plight of god for man, but there is some social resignation to the religious idolatry of the greater common to understand that the spirits and saints that befall the worshiper of clock part resources does not strike some common chord with the church. But the intersecting breeds of differences upon differences are such there can be no mention of the greater common to do disdain to the amateur occultist in his or her plight to accept the new words about the subject that god and the higher properties are but social monikers; aye, the luciferian in us must find that there is some tome about law that does not justify the greater law theorems that we are overwhelmed by the social ideas that Dionysus is but a heathen to the greater scheme about the magical picture; there is an extrapolation of the social that resides in the time mage to do some just experience to the darker accords, but only in the fashion. There need not be some greater tool of the heavens to disrupt the day other than the clock mechanisms that hang high in the phenomenal reality of the day, but this is merely an superstitious-acquaint.

Chapter 7: Magical objects and trinkets

Of the tithings to the time magic of the day that calls to the objects of our rooms we hold so dear, there are the obvious clocks and watches to do some justification to the exact amount upon which there can be some measure, thus time. But it is some hold about the expanse inside of us that grasps some greater accord to the server-like experience of certain clock pieces. Compasses namely, the chemistry about which remain a mystery to some, these holding-boxes about themselves that skew the eyesight to form some philosophy about the room, there is this to do some bidding to the greater scheme about the world map that time must resolve to the individual and society about space.

There is for some common understanding in the box about an object that measures some angle a sheer nostalgia. Boxes containing measuring tools can be quite beautiful and it is for some decent acceptance that these boxes are well kept - to the extent there *is* a trinket within, there! Looking, feeling, doing some service to the voice to announce a procedure at the tool - there are those things about us that cry out to our tools. The greater essences about our tools are our bodily wastes, our room-scum, the ambient smoke of the surrounding day; aye, there is the reality. But there is the cleanliness to the shining of a tool to objectify time and direction that does some justification to reject the old calculus that time is lost to measure and mark.

Of the schemes man and woman have borne, there is time magic in the sullenness that the void about the woman be not harmed. There is that taking away from a tool that the pointy parts stay clean or intentionally dirty from the likenesses of the waist, but clock objects on the belt can be drawn up socially to the extent that, aye, *drawn* to the hand is some timepiece and contortion of the thing to do justice to the pendulum. And it is here there is fault to the poet who has collected such time pieces, but fails to maintain them - the morally higher ground. The swinging of a pendulum with a dead clock is a joy of the eye, and it is seen that there is some living testament to the exposé of the common in its linking to the body, these clothes, this inherent and fashionable love-piece.

That the pendulum has done some grasping within the consciousness to detail the slow and listless dropping to a lower ground, there can be the experiment of gravity to quell the imagination that there ever was a weight on the persona to give some intentional and/or radical vision to the thing; there is a swing and the purchase of the air is simply not enough for a time mage to conquer the equestrian about the centaur of crawling hand and foot upon other clock surfaces. The mason. The careful drawing of the illuminated soul that has given some texture to a private building. There are such houses.

And it is that the philosophy of the technical society must wain when the artefacts are brought to question, ones responsible for a marking of notes or minutes that the second is restricted from the place-holder in the maths to do just circumstance to some folly about producing change to the social regular. I see that there is some great production in the factory-scale to do just notation to the striving-to-work, that inner-slavery of the body to work beyond the means without much comfort. But in our modern society, there is nothing but a relaxation and tension that can accompany the wisdom of the clock surfaces, thus we must strive to possess them privately. Integrating such technology tactically, there are the displacements of ammunition through the centuries to account for he position of the sun and the sneaking of the night. It is however that the ammunition that rests and is marked in the battlement by a careful measurement of time expires to the winds.

Where there is a violence to the time mage to rally for objects that should account for time, there is the striving to loosen the fear about the past, the future, the common moment, the latter some higher point to the scheme of the senses to do suggestible violence to proceed forward, but hardly is it that there is backtracking in the day (about the discreet) that there is some footing to acquire a less objectionable and, at the least, conflicting social qualm after another. It is the suggestible plot to undermine the intentions of one's inner-magnitude to regain the thing at all, some inner-plight that suggests the fascism about society does not weigh heavily on the spirit to entice one to combativeness. Thus, there is the instigation of the sorrow and suffering to find within the body and inner-heart mechanisms some deed that balances well with the forces of the phenomenal.

I see that there can be some clock part that may entice the consciousness, though it is not set to some complete thing to do a good service in and of itself. It is such that the taking of nutrition is to bring to some savant layer about the reality some greater thing than to ignore the life of survivability in the habits that there can be a new food source associated with an ordinary organ understood to give some second-nature reality another chance (within the body) that the time mage is balanced or wholeheartedly suggests to society a law argua that there is a need for reform about time. It can be that the time mage in his or her expanse is but a common nuisance indeed, but one with a good heart and clever intuition about the mechanical. Aye, there is protection for such a soul and there need not be but an accumulation of tools and meditations to understand the slips through time that exact some degree of common and granted subject some tolerance before exposé.

Advanced technology comes and goes in the environment in a way that we may be saddened when a favourite piece of our breaks or malfunctions to the extent there is a panic of sorts, to do good justice to abandoning or repairing the object. With a clock or watch, there are indeed specialists whom can analyse the state of the thing as a piece of costume jewellery, but it can be little known as to the effects of such a piece without dire consequences of the time mage and such an expert that could manifest as a friend or business partner. The inner-workings of sophisticated GPS watches for example are so bizarre in their beauty that symbols associated with various functions are still readily unknown and difficult to transcribe to a functional keyboard for a furthered examination. It is the testimony of the microscope that deters the time mage from their greater goals however, and the sciences must wain for the creativity in the span of the existence of certain advanced pieces of technology.

It is common in the sense that there is some sexual and expressive modality to consider time pieces that are inserted or ingested - drawn into the blood perhaps, but giving for some force a bitter and unknown direction. The body is such a powerful modality for the clock to entice that there is a failure of the enticed modality when considering time magic should the technologies raise to some stimulation without interest. It is such that the tiredness and the transportation amidst clock functionality such as that of the Philadelphia Experiment in its apprehensible colour-scheme is such that frequency is considered over quantity; the time mage is a traveling pioneer should there be some art to being lost in a map.

That there is equipment substantial to raise a battlement against naval games, there is the scientology of the markings that brings some calm to the notating pen. It is however a lost art for some to consider special uniforms and a lack of invasive time pieces that the science can emerge from the beckoning and harkened lists that form a criminal reform after another; law is within the naval instances such that time and the oceans are such a fearful moniker for the absurd that battlements must raise to a uniformed intrigue. Some common notes upon nations in specific may raise an interest in the traveling for the time mage, but there can be a stationary appreciation for a time mage who utilises natural postures and appreciates the animals about the society that are at a respective distance as to be considered by the eye. It is the ear that can reflect for some that the detonation of a timepiece causes such a warming conflict in the body as to generate a social worry unlike any other.

The devices of the time mage are so varied that the access to them must be loosened in the sciences for some, yet there is that contention that society is simply not allowing for the timepieces to be subject to the hands of children and adults in certain settings that there can be dismay when the senses fail to account for the tools' measure. It is apparent that clocks and watches, rings of special quality, swinging necklace pieces, pendulum watches, and higher-positioned clock towers, the *Lestat* of the latter powers to descend upon us by an uneasy authority to look to the heavens. It is however the inner-need to draw forth the common in us to not do contrived injustices to our society, our fellows, nor unto our technologies that we decay before the eyes of the social realms and individual expressions that we love and cherish.

Chapter 8: Teleport

For the requiem journey of the time mage, there is the teleportation in the act to consider. There can be before us some goal and ahead is some mechanism to which we may be able to reach with technique and equipment, but there are of course the ethics that challenge the animal to do *good* deeds in our travels. It is that hankering within to do some gruesome about the travel that war is omitted from a table and the relaxation about the society may resume. However benign the instigation to draw fire from a weapon amidst teleportation, there is the encapsulation of the *fine* to do some deed unto us that the social realms are not obliterated by our madness (beyond't the weaponry). In our skill to assess the mechanisms of the sequences before time and the physics of the matter, there is that meditation to the inner feelings that the body collapses and/or *breaths backwards* as though in the air before the body, but hardly *behind* the body. It is however to the perception of the brain and body that amidst a powerful teleport there is the consideration to move forward without collision unnecessary and yet that softness of the resolve of materials effected to some colossal social investigation as to *how* our appearance in some new region from afar could effect the greater mechanisms, it is indeed *teleport* to be considered as a skill rather than part of the regalia of the time mage.

The Mathematics of Time

For the philosophical, there is no time for the time mage to consider teleportation than to ponder whether such a thing resounds for its popularity in the sub-mechanical digressions of speech and language - that! To be ahead, there is some resort the backpedaling as to confront fear amidst teleportation, but there can be some common sense in the striving with one's wits and technology to return home.

The Mathematics of Time

For the time mage, there can be but the other skills mentioned throughout this work and other mechanical devices that there is a happiness rather than a lust in the machine - nay, for there is a dispute here; the time mage is just in teleportation and must refrain from acquiring much technology in unusual regions wherein the teleportation may arise and aye, there could be the colliding of physical bodies in space such that there is bizarre conflict between similar species and an ignorance for the others. Unlike Sartre's hell, that the other is some inane and due-hardy ignorance for the meat that rises from leather. *Leather* is for the time mage the ultimate material and food.

Teleportation is not simply reserved and the excitement amongst music can bring for the time mage some lack of sorrow in teleportation, but could result in *tremendous* mechanical failure of sophisticated parts. Engines, gasoline, pins, rotors, and other high-heat mechanical parts could endanger or fell a time mage amidst teleportation, but there is an unusual coolness to teleportation, that the casual movement of the time mage is observed instead. This is a thankful digression in the work, that there may be for us a treatise on time magic. And lo! It is done.

Absolvency

There are the notes on the time magic exposition that there is cause and effect, but there is real mechanism to the instances the time mage is bothered by the reality of the moniker.

There is sequence and edge; outlining the uniform mathematics is to the detriment of the machine.

There is the total collapse of the theatre without the

maintenance of consciousness to total the outlying just and/or bridal stops about the music.

Trinkets

There is the music.

Ridges

There is the excitement of the poise. The music is the gun in the battlement for there is the space that the exposé is but a lighted path.

Horus rises for the Luciferian in the post to do some battlement to Africa that there is a loss of sensation.

House upon house is the light.

Brigades

There is the insight.

Social reforms and the plight

The Mathematics of Time

For there is the silver, there is the end to the thinking spirit that time is space to absolve the fancy.

The Mathematics of Time

www.ingramcontent.com/pod-product-compliance
Lightning Source LLC
Chambersburg PA
CBHW070646220526
45466CB00001B/321